ORIOLE PARK BRANCH
DATE DUE 3-02

DEMCO 38-296

DISCARD

AMERICAN WOMEN OF SCIENCE

The Collective Biographies Series

Collective Biographies

AMERICAN WOMEN OF SCIENCE

Carole Ann Camp

Enslow Publishers, Inc.

40 Industrial Road	PO Box 38
Box 398	Aldershot
Berkeley Heights, NJ 07922	Hants GU12 6BP
USA	UK

http://www.enslow.com

To my daughters, Morgan and Heather

Library of Congress Cataloging-in-Publication Data

Camp, Carole Ann.
    American women of science / Carole Ann Camp.
        p. cm.—(Collective biographies)
    Includes bibliographical references and index.
    ISBN 0-7660-1538-6
    1. Women scientists—United States—Biography—Juvenile literature. [1.
Scientists. 2. Women—Biography.] I. Title. II. Series.
    Q141 .C1285 2001
    500'.82'0973—dc21
                                            00-011119

Printed in the United States of America

10 9 8 7 6 5 4 3 2 1

To Our Readers:
We have done our best to make sure all Internet addresses in this book were active and appropriate when we went to press. However, the author and the publisher have no control over and assume no liability for the material available on those Internet sites or on other Web sites they may link to. Any comments or suggestions can be sent by e-mail to comments@enslow.com or to the address on the back cover.

Illustration Credits: AP/Wide World Photos, pp. 30, 58 Copyright © 1972 by Paul Brooks. Reprinted by permission of Frances Collin, Trustee, p. 50; Corel Corporation, pp. 24, 64; Courtesy of Cold Spring Harbor Laboratory Archives, photo from Marcus Rhodes, p. 20; Courtesy of The Dupont Company, pp. 78, 82; Courtesy of Dr. Rosalyn S. Yalow, Veterans Affairs Medical Center, S.A. Berson Research Laboratory, New York, pp. 68, 75; Courtesy of the United States Department of Defense, p. 40; Enslow Publishers, Inc., p. 37; Regina Greenwood, Duxbury, Massachusetts, p. 56; Rensselaer Polytechnic Institute, New York, p. 86; Sophia Smith Collection, Smith College, p. 16; The MIT Museum, Cambridge, MA, p. 91; The Village Press, Dallou, Massachusetts, p. 10; Unisys Corporation, p. 46; University of California, San Diego, pp. 94, 100.

Cover Illustration: (Top left): Grace Murray Hopper, Courtesy of the United States Department of Defense, Shirley Ann Jackson, Rensselaer Polytechnic Institute, New York; (Bottom left): Barbara McClintock, Courtesy of Cold Spring Harbor Laboratory Archives, photo from Marcus Rhodes; Flossie Wong-Staal, University of California, San Diego.

Contents

Introduction

Science is the process of observing, identifying, classifying, describing, and trying to explain the world of nature. Since the beginning of time, humans have tried to understand the natural world. Some studied nature just out of curiosity. Others needed to uncover the secrets of the world around them in order to help humanity. In the earliest days, people who studied the heavens could predict when it was time to plant or harvest crops. People who studied the human body could help cure diseases or mend broken limbs. As civilization evolved, so did humans' understanding of the world around them. As colleges and universities grew, the field of science became subdivided into special areas, such as astronomy, physics, chemistry, and biology. Further distinctions evolved—astrophysics, physical chemistry, genetics, and geology. During the 1930s and 1940s, more sciences emerged, recombining and redefining older designations, like quantum mechanics and nuclear physics. Other sciences evolved as technology helped scientists observe smaller and smaller particles of matter through electron microscopes or farther and farther away through powerful telescopes. During the 1950s and 1960s, advancement in computer technology made it possible for scientists to make calculations that had been impossible before the computer.

Men and women have always contributed to the ever-expanding body of knowledge known as science. In the following chapters are the stories of ten women who have dedicated their lives to science and to our understanding of nature. Several of the women were on the cutting edge in their field. Florence Bascom introduced geology as a legitimate field of study for women. When Maria Goeppert-Mayer immigrated to the United States, she was one of the physicists leading the way in the new field of quantum mechanics. Chien-Shiung Wu was known as the queen of physics and an expert in nuclear fission. Her colleagues called Grace Murray Hopper "Grandma COBOL." Rachel Carson's writings set fire to the newly emerging field of environmental science.

These women experienced many obstacles set in their path by society and cultural norms. Florence Bascom was not admitted to a degree program at Johns Hopkins because she was a woman and had to sit behind a screen in classes so she would not distract the male students. Maria Goeppert-Mayer, Barbara McClintock, Stephanie Kwolek, and Rachel Carson had difficulty finding employment as scientists. Shirley Ann Jackson faced the isolation of being an African-American woman in an all-white male school. Rosalyn Yalow was not allowed to go to medical school because she is Jewish, and at the time she applied there existed a quota system for acceptance based on religion and ethnic background. Maria

Goeppert-Mayer, Chien-Shiung Wu, and Flossie Wong-Staal had to learn a new language and a new culture. Each of these women persevered. Their love of science and their dedication to their work carried them on.

Unfortunately, it took two world wars to change the prejudices against women in the fields of science and engineering in the major universities and industry. These prejudices started to change as women took men's places in colleges and the work place when the men were away fighting the war.

The women in this book are only a few of the women who were pioneers—opening science as a career option for women as well as contributing to humanity's curiosity about our natural world. In this group of women are many firsts. Florence Bascom was the first American geologist. Barbara McClintock was the first woman to receive the Nobel Prize in physiology and medicine on her own without being the member of a team. Maria Goeppert-Mayer was the first American woman to receive the Nobel Prize in theoretical physics. Grace Murray Hopper wrote the first compiler and subroutine for the computer. Rachel Carson started the environmental revolution. Chien-Shiung Wu was the first woman to teach at Princeton University. Rosalyn Yalow was the first woman educated in the United States to win the Nobel Prize in science. Stephanie Kwolek invented Kevlar®, a man-made organic fiber used in many industries. Shirley Ann

Jackson serves as the first woman president of a major science and engineering university. Flossie Wong-Staal is one of the most quoted scientists on the topic of HIV and AIDS research.

For these women, science was not only a way of life, it was their passion.

Florence Bascom

Florence Bascom
Geologist

"In those days [1890s], a young woman preoccupied with hammering rocks on country roads was stared at. Farmers drove her off their premises; cursed her as a trespasser;" "She was chased by bulls. But nothing daunted her." "A boy shouted, 'There goes the *Stone Lady*!'"[1]

Florence Bascom, the "Stone Lady", was born in Williamstown, Massachusetts, on July 14, 1862. Florence's father, John, a minister, taught at Williams College in Williamstown. Florence's mother, Emma Curtiss, joined many groups that fought for the rights of women. Florence was the youngest of six children, three of whom never lived to be adults. Florence's mother had a deep interest in science, especially botany. Emma Bascom encouraged her children to explore science and the natural world. Florence, a quiet child, spent much of her time with her father looking at the wonders of nature.

When Florence was twelve, her father accepted a position as president of the University of Wisconsin in Madison. As president, John Bascom helped the University of Wisconsin become one of the first colleges in the country to admit men and women equally.

Florence graduated from the Madison, Wisconsin, high school when she was fifteen. Then she started her college undergraduate studies at the University of Wisconsin. She earned three bachelor's degrees: a bachelor of arts and a bachelor of letters in 1882 and a bachelor of science in 1884.

During the following year, Florence Bascom taught at Hampton Institute for Negroes and American Indians in Virginia, returning home to Madison a year later to continue her studies. She received a master of arts degree in geology in 1887. The family moved back to Williamstown, Massachusetts, where John Bascom rejoined the faculty of Williams College. Florence Bascom taught Greek and physical geography at the local high school there. The end of the 1880s brought the Bascom family some financial difficulties.[2] To help relieve some of it, Florence Bascom decided to leave home and become self-supporting. She joined the faculty of Rockford College in Illinois where she taught courses in geology—the study of rocks and minerals, and chemistry—the study of matter.

Bascom wanted to go to Johns Hopkins University in Baltimore, Maryland, to study geology. At the time Johns Hopkins did not admit women to their graduate school. Following a special vote of the Board of Trustees, Bascom was allowed to take courses but without paying tuition. This made it possible for the trustees to claim that they did not and would not admit women to their school.

Although Johns Hopkins allowed her to attend classes, she was required to sit behind a screen so that the male students could not see her. It was thought that her presence would distract the men from their studies. Florence Bascom studied geology and pale-ontology with George Williams, a well-known geologist, from 1891 to 1893. *Paleontology* is the study of life that existed in early geologic history. Examples of these lifeforms can be found preserved in rocks and are known as fossils. In 1893, Bascom received a Ph.D. degree from Johns Hopkins. It was almost twenty years before Johns Hopkins conferred another Ph.D. degree on a woman. Several years later in 1896, after the establishment of Phi Beta Kappa, an honor society for students with outstanding grades, the Johns Hopkins chapter elected Florence Bascom as one of its first members.

Bascom left Johns Hopkins for Ohio State University where she taught undergraduate courses for two years. She wanted to do research, but time and opportunity to pursue her own interests were scarce because of her teaching responsibilities. In 1895, Bryn Mawr, a woman's college in Pennsylvania that had just established a graduate school for women, offered her a position on their faculty. Going to Bryn Mawr provided Bascom with the opportunity she wanted—to do more research. At the time, Bryn Mawr, as well as most colleges and universities, believed that women would not be interested in majoring in geology or working as a geologist. Bascom changed that perception.

During the year following her move to Bryn Mawr, Bascom also became the first woman hired by the United States Geological Survey, which provided maps for all of the land owned by the United States. Throughout her life and even in her retirement, she contributed to the study of the rock formations in southeastern Pennsylvania, Maryland, and New Jersey. For the survey, she studied the crystalline rocks in the mid-Atlantic Piedmont Province on the eastern edge of the Appalachian Mountains. She devoted every summer vacation from Bryn Mawr to gathering and studying rocks for the United States Geological Survey. Occasionally, she spent some of her summer vacations going to meetings with other geologists. In the summer of 1897, she attended the International Geological Congress in St. Petersburg, Russia.

While Bascom dedicated most of her time to teaching, she also worked to change people's attitudes about geology as a field of study. Geology was a relatively new field of study. She believed that women as well as men should have the opportunity to study in this field if they wanted to. When Bascom went to Bryn Mawr, geology courses were taught only as minor courses in other science majors, such as chemistry and biology. Three years later, geology became a new department. By 1901, Bascom had established geology as a major. She opened up the field of geology as a possible career choice for women. While teaching at Bryn Mawr and working for the United States Geological Survey, she also continued to do some of her own research. In 1901 she became the first woman to deliver a paper at the Geological Society of Washington.[3]

At the end of the nineteenth century, geology was still a relatively new science in the United States. The schools in Europe taught more advanced techniques for analyzing geologic forms than the schools in the United States. In 1906, Bascom, on leave from Bryn Mawr, studied crystallography with Dr. Victor Goldschmidt in Germany, one of the world's leading geologists. Bascom continued to study and do research. Soon Bascom became known in geological circles as an expert in crystallography, mineralogy, and petrography.

Crystallography is the study of the structure of crystals. *Mineralogy* is the study of minerals—how to identify and classify them. Mineralogy also includes discovering and testing the properties of different

Florence Bascom on a field trip (probably the Grand Canyon) in 1906. Bascom is second from front.

minerals, such as hardness. *Petrography* involves describing and classifying rocks. For example, in her dissertation, Bascom changed the classification of certain rocks. Other scientists had classified some rocks as sedimentary rocks, but she showed that the rocks were really from metamorphosed, or transformed, lava flows. Knowing how different rocks are formed helps scientists learn about the geologic history of an area.

In 1909, Bryn Mawr appointed Bascom to the paid position of full professor. By 1910 the geology department had graduate students from around the world. Many of these women graduated from Bryn Mawr with advanced degrees in geology. Several of them went on to lead remarkable careers in the field, all because Florence Bascom had opened geology up as a career for women. Creating a new department and a new major was not easy. There was much resistance. Ida Ogilvie, one of Bascom's students reflects: "Probably no one will ever know all the difficulties that she encountered, but little by little she achieved her purpose of making her department one of the best in the country."[4] Bascom believed that some of her best work was nurturing future women geologists, and she was proud of her accomplishment.[5]

While she worked at creating, expanding, and supporting the geology department of Bryn Mawr, she also edited the *American Geologist Journal* from 1896 to 1905. In addition to her many other firsts, she was designated as one of the country's leading geologists in the first edition of *American Men and Women of Science.* She became the first woman elected to the Council of the Geological Society of America in 1924 and its first woman officer in 1930.

For Florence Bascom, her life was her work, and her work was her life. She said, "This is the life, to plunge into the welcome isolation of the field, to return to the stimulating association of Bryn Mawr, to observe and in part to clear up geologic phenomena...."[6] She never married and did not participate in many, if any, social activities. For exercise and entertainment, she rode her horse, Fantasy, given to her by her uncle.

Bascom taught at Bryn Mawr until her retirement in 1928, when she moved back to western Massachusetts. She purchased a large farmhouse with land for her new horse, Starlight. Bryn Mawr still provided her with an office and laboratory space. After two years, of commuting back and forth to Bryn Mawr, she discovered that her memory was failing and that the field of geology had moved on. She left Bryn Mawr for the second time. This time never to return. At the end of her life, with a failing memory, she lived with her sister in rooms of the old family house in Williamstown. In 1945, two years after her sister died, Florence Bascom died at the age of eighty-three.

Barbara McClintock
Geneticist

At Cornell University in Ithaca, New York, in the 1920s, Barbara McClintock was growing Indian corn. As she planted and watered and weeded, her real goal was science, not farming. Each plant represented a special variety of corn that McClintock was observing.

One night there was a terrible storm. Rain poured down and brooks and rivers in the area flooded. Torrents of water ran down the hillsides tearing up trees and vegetation. In a small field Barbara McClintock worked nonstop to save her precious corn plants. Up to her ankles in water and working all night, she rescued each plant as it started to slide away in the mud. Despite the violence of the

Barbara McClintock

storm, she never hesitated to save her plants. This was typical of Barbara McClintock.[1]

Barbara McClintock was born on June 16, 1902, to Sara Handy and Dr. Thomas Henry McClintock of Hartford, Connecticut. Barbara had two older sisters and a younger brother. When Barbara was six years old, the family moved to Brooklyn, New York. Barbara was an independent child and had many opportunities to develop the qualities that would be helpful to her one day as a scientist. Scientists need to be able to focus on a problem or project for a long time without interruption. During summers spent on Long Beach, New York, Barbara took long walks alone. She spent much of her time reading or just sitting quietly thinking. Throughout her life, she would continue to enjoy these solitary activities.

Young Barbara was also a tomboy who loved to climb trees and play street games with the boys in the neighborhood. Even as a child, Barbara did not concern herself with society's rules. She persuaded her mother to allow her to wear bloomers—a style of pants—instead of the dresses that girls of her day were expected to wear. The McClintocks encouraged their children to follow their own interests and often let them skip school.[2]

During her high school years, Barbara discovered science. She was an original thinker and came up with unique ideas. "I would solve some of the problems in ways that weren't the answers the instructor expected," she said.[3] Throughout her life, she continued this pattern of not doing things the way everyone else did.

Barbara graduated from Erasmus Hall High School in 1919. Against much pressure from her friends and family, Barbara enrolled in college. She entered Cornell in 1919 intending to major in plant breeding and to study genetics—the science of heredity. However, women were not allowed to major in plant breeding because people believed if a "woman had to go out to talk to farmers about corn problems they [the farmers] would not listen."[4] So, she majored in botany—the study of plants.

Throughout her years in college, Barbara McClintock continued to think for herself. She freely ignored both the dress styles of the times and the ideas of her classmates. She chose to have short hair years before it became fashionable for women to cut their hair. She ignored the expected role of women students of her time, many of whom attended college with the main goal of finding a husband. She never married.

While studying occupied most of her time and energy, she had some other interests as well. She loved music and played the banjo in nightclubs around Ithaca, New York. However, as she became more and more focused on her research, she gave up her music. She was unable to study all day and stay up all night playing the banjo.

During college, McClintock decided to become a scientist, and biology became her life. McClintock graduated from Cornell in 1923 with a bachelor of science degree in botany. She continued at Cornell as a graduate student working on maize cytogenics. *Genetics* is the study of heredity—how traits are passed from one generation to another. For example, if both parents have blue eyes, their children will probably have blue eyes. *Cytology* is the branch of biology that studies cells through a microscope. Using maize, a form of corn with different-colored kernels, McClintock searched for links between chromosomes and heredity. *Chromosomes* are the tiny threadlike strands of DNA in the nucleus of the cell where the genes are. Each *gene* is responsible for a certain trait, like blue eyes or curly hair in humans.

In 1925, McClintock received a master's degree in botany. This degree was followed two years later by a Ph.D. in botany and genetics. By the time she completed her graduate studies, McClintock had taken all the courses in botany, cytology, genetics, and zoology that Cornell University had to offer.

In 1931, McClintock and another scientist, Harriet Creighton, published a very important research paper. They proved the theory of *recombination,* or *crossing over,* of genetic material. They showed that pieces of chromososmes actually trade places, moving pieces or entire genes from one chromosome to another. Crossing over explains why an offspring can be different from its parents. This important research contributed to Barbara McClintock's status as a geneticist.

Using maize, a form of corn, Barbara McClintock searched for links
between chromosomes and heredity.

During the summer of 1931 at the University of Missouri, McClintock studied maize chromosomes that scientists broke into pieces with X-rays. She noticed that the ends of these broken chromosomes eventually healed. The results of the healing, however, were mutations that caused different-colored offspring from the parent plants. A *mutation* is a change in the structure of a gene or chromosome that creates a new trait not found in the parents. McClintock was the first scientist to notice and report on these mutations. She wrote a series of papers describing her findings.

After graduation, McClintock continued doing research at Cornell University until 1932. She studied the ten chromosomes of maize and the genes each chromosome carried. However, Cornell did not offer her a permanent position. At the time very few colleges hired women as professors. Scientific research positions were even harder to find. Because scientists need money to support their work, McClintock went from job to job, supported by a variety of small grants. Over the next several years, she traveled from university to university, with frequent visits back to Cornell. The university still allowed her to have laboratory space and land on which to plant crops to use for her experiments.

From Missouri, McClintock went to the California Institute of Technology, in Pasadena, then briefly to Germany, and finally back to Cornell. In 1936, McClintock's friend, Lewis Stadler, invited her to join the staff as a research scientist at the University of Missouri. The university provided her with laboratory space, equipment, and a chance to work on her own research. In 1939 the Genetics Society of America elected her vice-president. However, her growing importance as a geneticist did not help her status at the University of Missouri. McClintock did not fit in at the conservative, male-dominated institution. In 1941 she left Missouri, saying, "It just means that there was no hope for a maverick like me to ever be at a university."[5]

In 1942 she joined the genetics team at Cold Spring Harbor, New York, sponsored by The Carnegie Institution. Here she finally found a place where she was truly happy. She had farmland for her crops, a laboratory for her experiments, and a place to live. McClintock loved her work. She spent twelve to sixteen hours a day, seven days a week, working in the cornfields or in her lab. She continued her experiments with maize, and she continued to publish papers about her work.

Barbara McClintock was gaining more recognition in the field of genetics. In 1944 she was the third woman ever elected to the National Academy of Science. In 1945, McClintock was the first woman elected to be president of the Genetics Society of America.

In 1951, during her time at Cold Spring Harbor, McClintock made a startling discovery. Her research led her to believe that some parts of the genes rearranged themselves on the chromosomes. Her discovery, later nicknamed jumping genes, contradicted the theory held by geneticists at the time. They believed that genes, arranged on chromosomes in fixed patterns—like beads on a string, did not move.[6]

McClintock's discovery announced in 1951 went unrecognized for nearly thirty years. Her idea was too radical, and very few scientists even understood what she was suggesting. McClintock did not give up. She believed in the truth of her work. Even without acceptance of her *jumping gene* theory, the scientific community respected her as a scientist. In 1970, McClintock was the first woman to receive the National Medal of Science.

Over the years other scientists began doing research that supported McClintock's theory. Biologists began to understand the importance of her work.[7] Three decades after her initial discovery, all the world was told through the Nobel Prize about Barbara McClintock's jumping gene theory. In 1983, McClintock, age eighty-one, received the Nobel Prize in physiology and medicine. She was the first woman to receive the prize for her own work and not as a member of a team. The Nobel Prize Committee announced that her work was "one of the two great discoveries of our times in genetics."[8]

McClintock also received many other awards throughout her distinguished career as a geneticist. She was awarded at least twelve honorary degrees, including ones from Harvard University in 1979 and Yale University in 1982. McClintock's dedication to her plants and her research carried her through many years of hard work. Even after her official retirement from Cold Spring Harbor in 1967, she continued to work on her research with genes and chromosomes until her death on September 2, 1992.

Maria Goeppert-Mayer
Physicist

Maria Goeppert-Mayer worked most of her life without ever receiving payment for her research skills and knowledge of physics. For decades she worked as a volunteer assistant professor at several universities and colleges. She did most of her Nobel Prize research because she thought that physics was fun.

Maria Goeppert was born on June 28, 1906, in Upper Silesia, then part of Germany now part of Poland. Maria was the only child of Friedrich and Maria Goeppert. Her father taught classes in pediatrics, the branch of medicine devoted to babies and small children. When Maria was four, the family moved to Göttingen in central Germany, where Maria's father had a teaching position at the university there. Maria enjoyed a happy childhood.

Maria Goeppert-Mayer

During her younger years, Maria attended a variety of public and private schools. Maria went to one of the few private schools that prepared girls to take the entrance exams for college. Maria's father wanted her to be more than a housewife.[1] Against the advice of her teachers, Maria took the college entrance exam a year early. Only five young women were among the hundreds of men who took the exam. All five women passed.

In 1924, Maria entered Göttingen University. In the early 1920s, Göttingen was a very famous place to study mathematics and physics. *Physics* is the study of matter and energy and how matter and energy interact. Many of the important scientists who started the new branch of physics called quantum mechanics, gathered in Göttingen during the 1920s and 1930s.

Quantum mechanics is the study of how the smallest things, like the parts of atoms, neutrons, protons, and electrons work and interact. Previously, some chemists studied how the electrons around the nucleus of atoms acted to form molecules. Some physicists studied the nucleus of atoms and how the various particles of the nucleus interacted with each other. However, the new area of quantum mechanics led chemists and physicists to work together. Besides physics and chemistry, the new science also included biology and astronomy. Some of the famous scientists who gathered in Göttingen during the 1920s included: Niels Bohr, Enrico Fermi, Robert

Oppenheimer, Werner Heisenberg, Erwin Schroedinger, Wolfgang Pauli, Linus Pauling, and Max Born.

Max Born was one of Maria's teachers. It was during one of Born's classes that Maria decided to change her major from mathematics to physics. In the world of physics and the development of quantum mechanics, Maria Goeppert was fortunate to be right in the middle of the new scientific discoveries.

Maria lived in an exciting college community. In addition, she was beautiful, enchanting, full of fun, and intellectually stimulating. Everyone was in love with her.[2] When her father died in 1927, Maria's mother, like many other widowed college professors' wives, took in boarders. Among the boarders at the Goeppert home was Joseph Mayer, a young chemist from California. He, like so many others, had come to work with the group of scientists at Göttingen University. On January 19, 1930, Joseph Mayer married Maria Goeppert.

While making plans for her wedding, Maria Goeppert wrote her dissertation. Using mathematics, she predicted that an electron orbiting an atom's nucleus would emit two photons—light packets—as the electron jumped to an orbit closer to the nucleus. Eugene Wigner, who later shared the Nobel Prize with her, described her dissertation as a "masterpiece of clarity and concreteness."[3] It was thirty years later before other scientists confirmed her predictions by experiments.

In 1930, Joseph and Maria Mayer moved to Johns Hopkins University in Baltimore, Maryland, where Joseph Mayer had a position teaching chemistry. During this time, the United States was in the middle of the Great Depression. Jobs were scarce for everyone, nearly one third of the people were unemployed. Colleges, in particular, were reluctant to hire two people from the same family.

The field of quantum mechanics was just beginning at Johns Hopkins. No one had a background in quantum mechanics equal to Goeppert-Mayer. Despite her experience and educational background, she had a difficult time finding a paying position as a physicist. She worked at small odd jobs. One job involved writing letters in German for a professor at John Hopkins. The university allowed her to teach some classes to graduate students, but never for money. Goeppert-Mayer enjoyed these opportunities to teach what she loved. She also wrote ten scientific papers and a textbook during this time. She also continued to do research in physics just for intellectual stimulation.[4]

During the summers of 1931, 1932, and 1933, Maria Goeppert-Mayer returned to Germany to work with her old friend and teacher, Max Born. She watched as the Nazis became stronger and stronger in Germany. The Nazi party, under the leadership of Adolf Hitler, began to invade other European countries. In an attempt to have a "pure race," the Nazis put Jews and other people they believed to be undesirable in concentration camps or killed them. Goeppert-Mayer loved Germany and was very upset about what was happening in her country. She chose to give up her German citizenship and to become an American citizen. She joined other German Americans to help German refugees fleeing Hitler.[5]

In 1933, Goeppert-Mayer gave birth to her first child, Marianne. In 1938, when she was about to have their second child, Peter, her husband, Joseph left Johns Hopkins for Columbia University in New York City. Again, Goeppert-Mayer had difficulty getting a job—the physics department at Columbia would not hire her. However, the chair of the chemistry department gave her a minor teaching job with an office and a title, but no money.

In 1941, Goeppert-Mayer received her first job offer from Sarah Lawrence College in Bronxville, New York and her first salary. However, she still continued to do volunteer work at Columbia. After the Japanese bombed Pearl Harbor and the United States entered World War II in December 1941, the United States government gathered many physicists together to work on war-related activities. Many of these scientists moved to the University of Chicago. These activities included the development of radar and the atomic bomb. Goeppert-Mayer joined the group, but remained in New York, and did research on the top-secret atomic bomb. Because she feared that the Germans would develop the bomb first, she did everything in her power to help the United States produce the first atomic bomb.

Maria Goeppert-Mayer managed the Substitute Alloy Materials project, (SAM) at Columbia. Eventually she became the unofficial scientific leader of the team. Her work with SAM gave her credibility as a scientist. She became known as an expert problem solver. Although she worked on projects related to the development of the atomic bomb, most of these bomb-related tasks were unsuccessful. She said later, "We failed. We found nothing, and we were lucky, because we didn't contribute to the development of the bomb, and so we escaped the searing guilt felt to this day by those responsible for the bomb."[6]

Following the war, many of the scientists who had gathered at Columbia moved to the University of Chicago to work with physicist Enrico Fermi. The Mayers joined the group. Once again, at the University of Chicago, she was a "voluntary professor," with no salary. She did not care, because she was with all of her old friends doing what she loved best, having fun with physics. The Chicago research group reminded her of the good times in Göttingen. She gave seminars, served on committees, helped hire faculty, advised graduate students, and helped develop the difficult graduate physics exam. In the first year that the University gave the exam, four future Nobel Prize winners and thirteen future members of the National Academy of Sciences took the test.

One of Goeppert-Mayer's former students, Robert G. Sachs, later became head of the Theory Division of the Argonne National Laboratory outside of Chicago and hired her as a senior physicist. She continued to do volunteer work at the University of Chicago because it was exciting. It was during this time that she developed her Nobel Prize-winning project.

The theory Goeppert-Mayer proposed that earned her the Nobel Prize, is very difficult to understand without some knowledge about the energy inside the nucleus of an atom. She used an analogy to explain her theory to her daughter, Marianne. She imagined couples dancing the waltz together. Think of many couples dancing around the room in concentric circles—circles within circles. "Each circle corresponds to an energy level. In addition to orbiting, though, each couple is also spinning like a top. Now suppose that while orbiting counterclockwise, some couples are spinning clockwise, some counterclockwise. Those spinning counterclockwise will find the dancing easier than those spinning clockwise...."[7] Her model of the nucleus is called *spin-orbit coupling*. Like the couples dancing, some parts of the nucleus are spinning in one direction, while other parts are spinning in the opposite direction.

Goeppert-Mayer made strides in atom research. The atom shown here is carbon, with six protons, six neutrons, and six electrons. An atom has a central nucleus of protons and neutrons that is surrounded by electrons.

In 1959, Maria and Joseph Mayer accepted professorships at the San Diego campus of the University of California. The family moved to the West Coast. Here Goeppert-Mayer was made a full professor with full pay, but it was too late. Shortly after moving, she suffered a terrible stroke at the age of fifty-seven. Although the stroke paralyzed her left arm, she continued to work on her research.

Finally, in 1963, the world recognized her achievements. She won the Nobel Prize for her work on the structure of nuclear shells. She discovered the way protons and neutrons spin and revolve within the nucleus of an atom. She was the first American woman to win a Nobel Prize in theoretical physics.

She received many awards and honorary degrees, including ones from Mount Holyoke College and Smith College. Annually, the American Physical Society awards a prize in Maria Goeppert-Mayer's honor to an outstanding woman physicist—The Maria Goeppert-Mayer Award—in recognition of her work.

Maria Goeppert-Mayer died of heart disease in 1972.

4

Grace Murray Hopper
Mathematician and Computer Scientist, Navy Admiral

Grace Murray Hopper earned many titles throughout her life. In the computer world and in the navy, she was affectionately called Amazing Grace. Some called her the Grand Lady of Software or Grandma COBOL. "She was a mathematician, computer scientist, social scientist, corporate politician, marketing whiz, systems designer, skillful manager, and programmer."[1]

Grace Murray was born in New York City on December 9, 1906. Her father, Walter Fletcher Murray, worked as an insurance agent. Grace's love of mathematics may have come from her mother, Mary Campbell van Horne Murray. Mary's father, John, Grace's grandfather, served as the chief civil engineer

Commodore Grace Murray Hopper, USN

for New York City. During his career, he laid out all of the streets for upper New York City.[2]

As a young girl, Grace attended private schools. The teachers at her school expected every student to read and write book reports on at least twenty books each summer. The family liked to go to Wolfeboro, New Hampshire, for their summer vacations. Grace enjoyed the quiet retreat in Wolfeboro where she could do her reading and writing without the interruptions of a busy New York City life.[3] During one of the summers in Wolfeboro, Grace met her future husband, Vincent Hopper, who also liked to vacation there.

From her father, Grace learned to follow her dreams and to achieve whatever she wanted. Her parents believed that males and females should have the same opportunities and education. She studied mathematics at Vassar College and was one of the top students there. Grace graduated with a bachelor of arts degree in mathematics, Phi Beta Kappa, in 1928. *Phi Beta Kappa* is an honor society for students with outstanding grades. She also received a Vassar College Fellowship to help pay for graduate school at Yale University. In 1930 she received her master's degree from Yale and married Vincent Hopper, an educator. While working on her Ph.D., she taught in the Department of Mathematics of Vassar College. In 1934 she became the first women to receive a Ph.D. in mathematics from Yale University. Another honor society, Sigma Xi, elected her to their membership.

In the early 1940s, Hopper taught mathematics at Vassar College and Barnard College. After the United States entered World War II, Hopper followed the military tradition of her family and enlisted in the Navy WAVES (Women Accepted for Voluntary Emergency Service). She graduated at the top of her class from midshipman's school and was commissioned a lieutenant. As part of her navy assignment, she worked for the Bureau of Ordnance Computation Project at Harvard University. This assignment changed her life.

Researchers at Harvard, under the leadership of Howard Aiken, were developing a machine that would do repetitious mathematical calculations that the armed forces desperately needed. For example, ship commanders needed these calculations so they could aim the big guns on their ships at the correct angle. The navy assigned Hopper to the Harvard project. Aiken and colleagues tested this machine, called the Mark I, in January 1943. This early computer could do three additions every second and store seventy-two words. When Hopper reported for duty on the first day, Aiken asked her to make the Mark I calculate the "...coefficients for the interpolation of the arc tangent by next Thursday,"[4] which she did by creating a program for the machine to follow. Hopper was only the third person ever to program or code the Mark I to do a calculation.

This first real operating computer filled a large room and, when operating, made a considerable noise. Hopper and her team had to keep the Mark I both running—it constantly broke down—and calculating numbers for the navy. Although it was a very hectic time, Hopper fell in love with computers.[5] In addition to the daily frantic routine, Hopper began to write one of the first computer manuals. Harvard University Press published the five-hundred-page book called, *A Manual of Operation for the Automatic Sequence Controlled Calculator* in 1946.

When World War II ended in 1945, work continued on the Mark II. During the building of Mark II, the machine stopped suddenly. A moth had flown inside the Mark II and caused it to stop. Hopper pulled the moth out of the machine with a pair of tweezers and taped it into the logbook. That moth is said to be the first computer "bug." The first computer bug is still on display at the Naval Museum at the Naval Surface Weapons Center in Dahlgren, Virginia.[6] Today a bug is a mistake or problem in a computer program or equipment.

At the end of the war, Hopper stayed in the Naval Reserves and joined the Harvard faculty as a research fellow in engineering sciences at the Applied Physics Computation Laboratory. During the war, Grace and her husband had not lived together for many years. Her marriage ended as the war ended.

Hopper enjoyed working with computers. She wanted everyone, not just scientists and the military, to have fun with computers. The people she worked with told her that her idea of computers for the general public was crazy. However, she never let comments like "it can't be done" stand in her way.[7] She focused on her vision. Her coworkers did not share her vision, so she moved from academics to industry. In 1949 she left Harvard to work as a senior mathematician for the Eckert-Mauchly Computer Corporation, which later became Remington Rand and then Sperry Rand Corporation.

Computers used instructions (called programs) that are actually in the form of binary numbers. Programming a computer in these numbers was difficult and tedious. Hopper wanted the process to be easier. She wanted an interface so that more people could easily write programs for computers. She also wanted computers to be programmed using letters and real words instead of numbers. She believed the key to getting computers into the hands of ordinary people was to create computer languages that were easy to use and written in English, not in the numerical form called "machine language." Her coworkers again told her that it was impossible for a computer to read words. After a year of frustration with her managers, they finally gave her space and personnel to work on her idea.

Hopper wrote the first program that told the computer how to translate code in letters and symbols into the language the machine understood. This program, called a compiler, created a technological revolution. She also created subroutines, a set of computer instructions that the computer uses over and over again. When the computer needed one of these subroutines, it could access it with a call number. Hopper developed the computer language that later became known as FLOW-MATIC.[8]

She and her staff designed the computer so that it could understand twenty statements in English. Hopper published her first paper on compilers in 1952. A compiler is a program that translates the instructions written by people into the "machine language." FLOW-MATIC was a first step toward the development of COBOL. COBOL is a computer language used in business for business people— Common Business Oriented Language. Using COBOL, people in the business world can easily program computers to do boring repetitious calculations. They did not have to know how the insides of the computer worked or how to program the computer in machine language. COBOL used everyday words like ADD and SUBTRACT, SAVE and COPY. Hopper is called Grandma Cobol because her FLOW-MATIC Language was COBOL's direct ancestor.

Hopper continued to work as a systems engineer and Univac director of Automatic Programming Development for Remington Rand. She helped design the first large-scale electronic computer called UNIVAC—Universal Automatic Computer, the first

Grace Murray Hopper is shown here with UNIVAC, the first large-scale electronic computer she helped design.

computer for sale in 1950. It processed information a thousand times faster than the Mark I.

In 1966 the navy asked her to resign from the reserves because she had served longer than the allowed time. However, the navy soon found that it needed her computer skills and asked her to return to temporary duty for six months. They asked her to develop a standard usage of COBOL which became known as the *American Standard of COBOL*. She helped lead the effort to standardize COBOL and compilers. Her work eventually led to national and international standards for most programming languages.

Hopper left Remington-Rand and returned to active duty as the director of the Navy Programming Languages Group. In 1983 the navy promoted Hopper to commodore at a ceremony at the White House, a title later changed to admiral. She is one of the few women admirals in the history of the United States Navy. At seventy-nine years old, she was the oldest person serving the military on active duty. The navy celebrated her second retirement from the navy on board the USS *Constitution* in Boston Harbor. The Department of Defense awarded her the Distinguished Service Medal, the highest award given by the department. In her honor, the navy created The Grace Murray Hopper Service Center, a data-processing center. Throughout her distinguished career, she received many awards and honors including over forty honorary degrees.

She joined Digital Equipment Corporation at the age of eighty as senior consultant and worked with them for four years. Hopper said that she felt that her greatest contribution had been "all the young people she had trained."[9]

She traveled widely on lecture tours. She said in one of the famous quotes from her lectures, "the most damaging phrase in the language is, 'We've always done it this way.'"[10]

Grace Hopper died on January 1, 1992, and was buried with full naval honors at Arlington National Cemetery. After her death, she was elected to the National Women's Hall of Fame and the United States Navy named a guided missile destroyer after her, the USS *Grace Hopper*.

Rachel Carson

Marine Biologist, Environmentalist, Writer

In 1958, Olga Huckins called her friend Rachel Carson for help. Rachel Carson was a famous writer and a scientist. The Huckins family owned a bird sanctuary in Duxbury, Massachusetts. The town had tried to kill mosquitoes by spraying a chemical, called DDT, over the marshes around Duxbury. Mrs. Huckins told Rachel Carson that not only was DDT killing the mosquitoes, but it was also killing the birds as well. State officials had insisted that the chemical was not harmful to birds. Olga Huckins wanted Carson to help her report the incident to the federal government. Carson investigated the use of pesticides. As a result of her research, she became concerned about the effects pesticides had on

Rachel Carson

animals, humans, and the environment. After four years of careful research, Carson wrote her most famous book, *Silent Spring.* It started a revolution. An editorial in a newspaper said: "A few thousand words from her and the world took a new direction."[1]

Rachel Carson was born on May 27, 1907, to Maria and Robert Carson in Springdale, Pennsylvania. Robert Carson worked for the power company and as an insurance salesman. He also invested in real estate. One of his purchases was a sixty-five-acre farm in Pennsylvania near the Allegheny River. Maria Carson, a lover of nature, taught her three children, Marian, Robert, and Rachel to love nature as well. She taught them the names of plants and animals. They learned how to recognize birds by their songs. The young Carson children spent many hours in the woods, listening to and learning about nature.

Even as a young child, Rachel, the youngest in the family, dreamed of becoming a writer. She believed that when she grew up, her dream would come true. When she was ten years old, she submitted her first story to *St. Nicholas,* a popular magazine for children. "A Battle in the Clouds," a story about an airplane pilot in World War I, was the beginning of her writing career. She earned $10 for her first story. During the following two years, she won three more writing prizes for her stories. By the time Rachel was fourteen, she was well on her way to achieving her dream. She graduated from Parnassus

High School in Parnassus, Pennsylvania, in 1925. Throughout her high school years, her teachers encouraged her to write.

In the fall of 1925, Rachel Carson entered Pennsylvania College for Women and majored in writing. She wrote stories for the college newspaper, *The Arrow,* and for a literary magazine, *The Englicode.* In addition to her studies, Carson had time to participate in many sports like basketball, baseball, and field hockey. She was the goalie on a winning field hockey team.

During Carson's second year in college, a major event happened in her life. The college required that all students take at least one year of science. Carson took a biology class. After a year in this biology class, Carson changed her major from writing to zoology. At the time she feared that she would have to give up her dream of becoming a writer.[2] Instead, she found that she had a wonderful subject for her writing—the world of nature.

After graduating with honors at the age of twenty-two in 1929, Carson spent a summer working at the Marine Biological Laboratory on the Massachusetts coast. Living and working beside the ocean was another turning point in Carson's life. She had lived all of her younger life in the woods of Pennsylvania. Now the ocean provided her with new areas to explore. She spent many hours watching and studying the marine creatures in their natural habitat. She continued her studies in marine zoology at

Johns Hopkins University. While working on a project for her master's degree, she taught at Johns Hopkins summer school and the University of Maryland. During 1930, Carson's father experienced financial trouble and Robert and Maria Carson went to live with their daughter in Baltimore.

In 1932, Carson received a master's degree in marine zoology. Finding employment as a marine biologist was difficult at this time because of the Great Depression, a period in U.S. history of extremely high unemployment among other economic hardships. Jobs of any kind were very scarce. Women, in particular, could not find work—especially in the field of science. Carson continued teaching part-time at the University of Maryland. When her father died in 1935, she knew she needed more money to support her mother and herself. The United States Bureau of Fisheries in Washington D.C. hired her to write a series of radio broadcasts on marine life. In 1936 she took an exam for the position of junior aquatic biologist at the Bureau of Fisheries. She received the highest score on the test and the bureau offered her the job. Carson was the second woman ever hired by the Bureau for something other than secretarial work.[3]

With the encouragement of Elmer Higgins, head of the Division of Scientific Inquiry at the bureau, Carson submitted an article entitled "Undersea" to *The Atlantic Monthly* magazine. It was published in September 1937. Carson later expanded "Undersea" into a full-length book called *Under the Sea Wind,* published in 1941. In this book Carson wanted to give the reader an appreciation of the creatures of the sea. She hoped that by understanding the sea, people might be able to view human life differently.[4]

Although *Under the Sea Wind* went unnoticed and unread, Carson worked diligently as a marine biologist and earned promotions regularly. In 1946 she rose to the position of aquatic biologist. During this time she continued to write. Her articles appeared regularly in the *Baltimore Sun* newspaper. In 1950 she won the George Westinghouse Science Writing Award.

In 1951 she gained wider recognition when "The Sea Around Us" appeared in *The New Yorker* magazine as a series and was later published as a book. The book was an amazing success and won the National Book Award. Following the popularity of *The Sea Around Us, Under the Sea Wind* was republished. It also became a best seller. Rachel Carson, the shy marine scientist, was now an internationally famous writer. She continued to win a variety of awards and prizes. In 1952 she was the first woman to win the Henry G. Bryant Medal from the Philadelphia Geographical Society. She also received honorary doctorates from Drexel Institute of Technology, Oberlin College, and Chatham College.

In 1952, after the enormous success of her two books, Carson resigned from the Fish and Wildlife Service. She bought some land on the coast of

Maine. She planned to devote the rest of her life to her own research and writing. In 1955 she published *The Edge of the Sea*, another best seller. Carson's books introduced the general public to the natural world and to the science of nature in a gentle, easy-to-read style. As Carson's fame spread, she lectured around the country on a variety of topics related to the environment. In 1956 she received the Achievement Award from the American Association of University Women.

In response to concerns that people like her friend, Olga Huckins, were raising about the use of pesticides on the environment, Carson began to collect information from other scientists and the press related to the use of pesticides. DDT (Dichloro-Diphenyl-Trichloroethane) is one of the chemical pesticides many cities and towns used to kill mosquitoes. When towns used widespread spraying, other animals, especially birds, died. She had files and files of reports about how different chemicals used in pesticides were killing birds and fish. She could not be quiet about what she was learning, so she began writing *Silent Spring*. In 1962 *Silent Spring* was published as a serial in *The New Yorker* magazine. It fueled the newly rising environmental revolution. She wrote: "It is not possible to add pesticides to water anywhere without threatening the purity of water everywhere...."[5]

Silent Spring changed the course of history. More and more people became aware of the environment

In 1958 Rachel Carson investigated the use of pesticides on the marshes around Duxbury, Massachusetts. After four years of careful research, Carson wrote her most famous book, *Silent Spring.*

and started to make changes in their lifestyles. Unfortunately, change does not come without a struggle. Carson's book started a major controversy. She linked pesticides that companies had said were safe with cancer, birth defects, and death of humans and animals. Big chemical companies argued about the facts in the book. After the book was published, many other groups attacked Carson, calling her a "hysterical woman."[6] In spite of what the public believed, Carson was not calling for the total elimination of pesticides, she was only asking that people use pesticides responsibly. She wanted people to realize that uncontrolled use of pesticides could pollute the whole planet.

Not all criticism was negative. Many people applauded her efforts. After reading *Silent Spring*, President John F. Kennedy asked the Science Advisory Committee to study the use of pesticides. The committee supported Carson's findings, but the government did not ban the general use of DDT until 1972.

Unfortunately, Carson did not live to see DDT banned. She died of cancer at the age of fifty-seven on April 14, 1964. After her death, *The Sense of Wonder*, a book she had written for her grandnephew, was published in 1965. Almost twenty years later, the nation awarded her the President's Medal of Freedom.

Chien-Shiung Wu

6

Chien-Shiung Wu
Experimental Nuclear Physicist

Soon after Chien-Shiung Wu started to work at Princeton, the scientists designing the atom bomb, later known as the secret Manhattan Project, asked her to join them at Columbia University in New York. Wu was happy to do anything she could that would help free China from the Japanese.

Chien-Shiung Wu was born on May 31, 1912, in Liuhe, a small town near Shanghai, China. Chien-Shiung means *Courageous Hero* in Chinese. Chien-Shiung's father, Wu Zhongyi, hoped that his daughter would become a courageous hero. He had participated in the revolution of 1911, which brought down the Manchu dynasty. He wanted a better quality of life for the Chinese people. Both of Chien-Shiung's parents believed that females as well as males should have an education. To help realize their dreams, Chien-Shiung's father started a school for young girls. In this school the teachers encouraged girls to read and explore. When she was a girl, Chien-Shiung's parents hoped that she would grow up to be a scientist.

Chien-Shiung's father, the school principal, and her mother, a teacher, believed that girls should not have their feet bound. Foot binding was an ancient Chinese custom that kept girls' feet from growing. In the beginning of the 1900s, only progressive parents opposed the ancient customs. Chien-Shiung's mother, Fan Fahua, urged other mothers to stop binding their daughters' feet.

At age nine, Chien-Shiung graduated from her father's school and went to school in Suzhow, 50 miles inland from Shanghai. In this school, the Soochow Girls' School, she learned English. Many professors, visiting from colleges in the United States, lectured at this school. From these lectures Chien-Shiung learned about western culture. The high school provided two choices of courses— teacher training and academics. She chose teacher training because she knew she would be able to get a teaching position when she graduated. She soon discovered that the students in the academic classes took more mathematics and science classes than she was allowed to take. At night she borrowed math and science books from her classmates. She read them all and taught herself mathematics, physics, and chemistry.

In the process she discovered that she liked physics more than anything else.

Because she did not have adequate preparation, she was reluctant to enroll in math and science classes in college. Her father encouraged her by giving her books on advanced math, physics, and chemistry the summer before she went off to college. Later she said, "If it hadn't been for my father's encouragement, I would be teaching grade school somewhere in China now."[1]

At the National Central University in Nanking, she took all the physics and math courses offered for the bachelor of science degree. She was the top student in all of her classes. During the 1930s, Japan tried to invade and take over China. Following in her father's footsteps, Chien-Shiung became part of the student underground movement in support of China. She organized a boycott of Japanese goods and led many nationalist demonstrations. She even spoke with General Chiang Kai-shek, the Chinese leader, and urged him to stand firm against the Japanese. She was able to do this because she was part of a student demonstration at his house.

Many of her professors in college encouraged Chien-Shiung to pursue further degrees in science. She wanted to go to the United States to do graduate work in physics. Her parents encouraged her because they were afraid for her physical safety if she stayed in China because of the Japanese. After graduation from the National Central University in 1934, she spent a year doing research in X-ray crystallography at the National Academy of Sciences in Shanghai. Her instructor, who had earned her Ph.D. from the University of Michigan, urged Chien-Shiung to go to the United States and to the University of Michigan. Chien-Shiung left China in 1936 but enrolled at the University of California at Berkeley. In 1937, Japan invaded China. World War II followed. Chien-Shiung never saw her family again.

The Berkeley campus provided many opportunities for research in nuclear physics. Several famous physicists worked there. Chien-Shiung Wu fit in easily. She worked with Emilio Segré, who later won the Nobel Prize for Physics in 1959. As in her previous schools, she earned the highest grades in all of her courses.

In her doctoral thesis she studied what happens when the nucleus of the atom of uranium splits. This splitting process called *fission* occurs when a neutron moves at a very high speed and hits the nucleus of an atom. During the collision, the nucleus splits into parts and two or three neutrons. All these particles move away from each other at high speeds. In the process, they hit other nuclei. When many nuclei split in a short time, an explosion occurs, producing many more particles, often called an atomic explosion. If these fissions are controlled and made to occur over a longer period of time, we have the steady reaction conditions required in a nuclear power plant. In 1940 Wu received a Ph.D. in physics from Berkeley. Part of her thesis was not made public until the end of World War II. It was sent to Los Alamos National Laboratories, where other scientists were trying to develop the atomic bomb.

Wu was a very precise and creative experimenter and rarely made errors in her measurements.[2] Wu believed that physics was not only a job, but it was a way of life. She totally dedicated her life to her work. Emilio Segré said, "Wu's willpower and devotion to work are reminiscent of Marie Curie, but she is more worldly, elegant, and witty."[3] The physics community came to respect Wu as an expert on nuclear fission.

During her time at Berkeley, she met and married Dr. Luke Yuan, another physicist studying there. They had one son, Vincent, also a physicist. Despite her success as a nuclear physicist, the University of California at Berkeley did not offer her a position on their faculty. She and her husband left California for the East Coast. She became assistant professor in physics at Smith College, a women's college, in Northampton, Massachusetts. Her husband worked in Princeton, New Jersey, at the RCA Research laboratories. They visited each other on weekends and school vacations. After a year at Smith, Princeton University asked her to join their faculty. She became the first woman to teach at the all-male university.

In 1944 she joined the staff of the Division of War Research at Columbia University in New York City, working on the development of the atom

Chien-Shiung Wu worked on the "Manhattan Project," which was a confidential project begun by the United States government in 1942 to create the atomic bomb. On August 6, 1945 the United States dropped the first atomic bomb used in warfare on the city of Hiroshima in Japan.

bomb. The research team tried to find ways to produce large amounts of the specific radioactive isotope of uranium needed in the production of the atomic bomb. Wu's task was to design sensitive instruments to detect radiation during the bomb development process.

At the end of the war, Columbia University appointed Wu as research associate. A few years later, in 1952, she became an associate professor of physics. During these years, she did several experiments on Enrico Fermi's theory. His theory was that one of the types of particles that flies out of the nucleus in radioactive decay is a high-speed electron, called a beta particle. Scientists up until this point had only been able to find slow-moving electrons. Through careful experimentation, Wu proved that Fermi was right. Wu, along with Steven Maszknowski, wrote a book called *Beta-Decay*, which is still a classic in nuclear physics.

In 1956, Wu started her most famous work on the Law of Conservation of Parity. The conservation of parity was a law that the scientific community had accepted as true for at least thirty years. Two Chinese-American physicists, Tsaung Dao Lee and Chen Ning Yang, saw evidence that caused them to question the law. They asked Wu to design an experiment to verify their observations.[4]

Wu conducted the experiment at the National Bureau of Standards in Washington, D.C. Wu's experiments proved the law of conservation of parity was not true for some parts of the atom. On January 16, 1957, Columbia held a press conference to announce that a basic law in physics had been disproved. Wu's findings shook the scientific community. Lee and Yang won the 1957 Nobel Prize for Physics for their theory, but Chien-Shiung Wu was not included in the team. Many people, including Wu, were disappointed at this decision.

Wu's skill as a precise and exacting experimenter led other scientists to seek her out for their work. Toward the end of her career, she conducted research on sickle-cell anemia using advanced biophysics techniques.

Wu returned to China in 1973. By then all of her family and most of her friends had died.

Throughout her career, Wu won many awards. As early in her career as 1947, *Industrial Research* magazine selected her as their *Scientist of the Year.* Columbia designated her as one of their all-time Teacher-Researcher Greats. In 1958 she received the first honorary doctorate Princeton had ever bestowed on a woman. Other honorary degrees came from Harvard, Yale, and Smith College. Wu was the first woman to receive the Comstock Award from the National Academy of Sciences. She won the Chi-Tain Culture Foundation of Taiwan award and gave the prize money to the Chin Institute of America for scholarships for Chinese students. In 1976, Wu received the National Medal of Science award from President Ford. *Newsweek* called her the "Queen of

Physics," others the first lady of physics research.[5] In addition to her work in physics, Wu was also an inventor with patents on at least five inventions, one related to the detection of radiation.[6]

She continued working at Columbia University until her retirement in 1981. Chien-Shiung Wu died of a stroke in 1997.

Rosalyn Sussman Yalow

Rosalyn Sussman Yalow
Medical Physicist

On January 1, 1995, Rosalyn Yalow suffered a stroke. When the paramedics took her to the hospital, they did not take any identification papers or insurance cards with her. The closest hospital was afraid that she did not have enough money or insurance to pay for treatment, so they sent her to the municipal hospital. Rosalyn Yalow, a Nobel Prize winner in medicine, almost died.[1]

On July 19, 1921, Rosalyn Sussman was born into the family of Clara Zipper and Simon Sussman. Her mother had come to America from Germany when she was four. Her father was a native New Yorker. The family lived in the Jewish section of the lower East Side of New York. Rosalyn continued to live in the same community throughout her life, except for a few years of graduate study in Chicago.

When she was a little girl, Rosalyn was a determined child.[2] Her mother said that even as a young child, Rosalyn had a competitive spirit.[3] Her family was poor and did not have much money to spend on books. Rosalyn's brother, Alexander, went to the library weekly to get new books for Rosalyn to read.[4]

In junior high school, Rosalyn found that she loved mathematics. In high school, she discovered another love, chemistry. She graduated from Walton High School in 1937 at the age of fifteen and entered Hunter College, a private college renowned for their training of women scientists. Professors Herbert Otis and Duane Roller of Hunter College introduced Rosalyn to physics. In the 1930s, scientists around the country were engaged in developing a new area of physics called nuclear physics. In spite of her earlier intention to seek a career in medicine, Rosalyn decided to major in physics. She enjoyed the excitement found in this new area of science. During her second year in college, she read a book by Eve Curie, the daughter of Madame Marie Curie, the famous French woman scientist. Marie Curie became Rosalyn Yalow's hero. During her junior year in college, she attended a lecture about nuclear fission given by Enrico Fermi. Her heart was set. Although her parents wanted her to be an elementary school teacher, she wanted a career in physics. She graduated from Hunter College in January 1941, with majors in physics and chemistry.

Within the field of nuclear physics, another new area opened—nuclear fission. Nuclear fission was not only required for making weapons of destruction; the discoveries could also be used in other ways, such as in medicine. Remembering her earlier desire to go into medical research, Rosalyn wanted to combine what she had learned in physics with medicine. She wanted to go to medical school, but many medical schools did not accept Jewish men or women to study medicine.[5] At this time there existed a quota system for acceptance based on religion and ethnic background. A friend helped her get a job as a secretary at Columbia University in New York, where she would be allowed to take courses as an employee of Columbia. Before she could take the courses, however, she decided instead to go to the University of Illinois as a graduate student in the engineering school. She was the only woman in a class of four hundred students. No women had been admitted to the engineering school at the University of Illinois since World War I. By the end of 1941, things had changed for the United States and for Rosalyn. The United States entered into World War II. Men were needed to fight in the war. Women took their places in colleges and in the workforce.

Rosalyn met Aaron Yalow on her first day at the University of Illinois in 1941. A year later she earned her master's degree. The following year, while continuing to study at the University of Illinois for her Ph.D. in nuclear physics, Aaron and Rosalyn married. When she finished her Ph.D. in 1945, she moved back to New York City without her husband who was still working on his thesis.

Rosalyn Yalow took a position at the Federal Telecommunications Laboratory. She was the first woman engineer they had ever hired. At the end of World War II, the group she worked with left New York. She, however, decided to leave the team and stay in New York City. She joined the faculty at Hunter College where she taught physics to classes of returning veterans. Unfortunately, Hunter College was not a research institution. By then, her husband had joined her and had taken a position in medical physics at Montefiore Hospital in the Bronx. Her husband introduced her to Dr. Edith Quimby, also a medical physicist. Rosalyn Yalow worked in Quimby's laboratory as a volunteer to gain experience in the medical applications of radioisotopes.[6] *Radioisotopes* are types of atoms that emit radiation.

By 1947, in order to keep working on her research, she joined the staff at Bronx Veteran's Administration Hospital. She also continued to work full time at Hunter College. With very little equipment and even less money, Yalow and several others working at the hospital were able to do research in many different medical areas. The Veterans Administration (VA) recognized the value of their research and decided to offer radioisotope services in several of its hospitals around the country. The Bronx VA hospital was one of the first hospitals in the United States to support Radioisotope Services.

In 1950, Yalow left Hunter College to work full time on her research at the hospital. Here she met and began working with Solomon Berson. She soon gave up working with other colleagues and worked only with him. This partnership lasted until Berson's death twenty-two years later. The team of Berson and Yalow became famous throughout the medical research community. Some of their first work included using radioisotopes to diagnose thyroid disease. They soon discovered how they could trace the flow of insulin as it circulates around the body in people with diabetes. During these years Rosalyn gave birth to Benjamin, born in 1952, and Elanna, born in 1954. The family moved to a new house in Riverdale, New York, less than a mile from the hospital.

In 1959, Berson and Yalow developed the first use of radioimmunoassay (RIA). RIA is a way to find very small amounts of chemicals in the body, in tissues, and in fluids. It is such a sensitive process that one could use it to detect a sugar cube in a lake.[7] Their work changed the study of diseases. Using RIA helps doctors detect many different diseases. It is possible to screen blood for hepatitis, determine effective doses of drugs, or test for the correct hormone levels in couples with fertility problems. Although Yalow never went to medical school to study medicine, she learned about medicine through her research and through collaboration with Berson.

In 1968, Berson left the VA hospital in the Bronx to take a position as chair of the Department of Medicine at the Mount Sinai School of Medicine. Four years later Berson died of a heart attack at age fifty-four. Yalow never forgot her partner and colleague. She renamed her research laboratory the Solomon A. Berson Research Laboratory. She said she did that so his name would appear on all of the papers she published. She did not want anyone to forget him.[8]

Yalow worked long hours in her lab, often spending more than one hundred hours a week there. Her lab produced hundreds of research articles—sharing their findings with other researchers.

In 1975 the National Academy of Sciences elected Yalow into their membership. That same year she received the A. Cressy Morrison Award in Natural Sciences from the New York Academy of Sciences. In 1976 she was the first woman to receive the Albert Lasker Basic Medical Research Award— highest science award in the United States.

One year later Yalow was the first American-educated woman to win a Nobel Prize in science and the second woman to win it in medicine. She shared the prize with Roger Guillemin of the Salk Institute and Andrew Schally of the Veterans Administration Hospital in New Orleans.

Dr. Rosalyn S. Yalow was the first American-educated woman to win a Nobel Prize in science and the second woman to win it in medicine.

Rosalyn Yalow holds over fifty honorary degrees from colleges and universities all over the country. In 1988 she received the United States' science award, the National Medal of Science.

A year after her retirement from the Bronx VA Hospital in 1991, Yalow's husband, Aaron, died after forty-nine years of marriage.[9] On New Year's Day, 1995 Yalow suffered a severe stroke. Less than two years later, Rosalyn Yalow returned to work to continue her remarkable career as a medical physicist.

8

Stephanie Louise Kwolek
Chemist

Few people realize that a woman invented Kevlar,[®] a material five times stronger than steel. Kevlar is used in bullet-resistant vests and has saved the lives of hundreds of police officers and soldiers. The initials S. L. on the patent for Kevlar belong to Stephanie Louise Kwolek, one of the DuPont Company's outstanding chemists.

Stephanie Louise Kwolek was born in New Kensington, Pennsylvania, on July 31, 1923. She was the oldest child of John and Nellie Zajdel Kwolek. John Kwolek earned his living working as a mold maker in a local foundry. Stephanie's father loved being in the outdoors exploring nature. He took Stephanie and her younger brother on nature hikes to collect leaves, flowers, seeds, and other things of

Stephanie Louise Kwolek

nature. Stephanie and her father spent many happy hours sorting and arranging these natural treasures into scrapbooks. In later years, when reflecting on her childhood, Stephanie recalls, "My father was a naturalist by avocation...I remember spending an awful lot of time with my father, roaming through the woods, collecting wildflowers and seeds and making scrapbooks of them."[1]

Stephanie's mother, Nellie, taught her how to sew, knit, and do other kinds of needlecrafts. From this early beginning, Stephanie developed a special interest in fabrics and different kinds of cloth and material. As Stephanie grew older, she could not decide if she wanted to be a scientist or a fashion designer. She loved science and anything to do with sewing equally.

When Stephanie was ten years old, her father died, leaving her mother with two small children to care for. Nellie Kwolek found work at the Aluminum Company of America. Life was difficult for the family during the Great Depression in the 1930s as it was for many families in America then. In spite of the financial difficulties, Stephanie's mother encouraged Stephanie to go to college.

Stephanie Kwolek graduated from high school in 1942 and enrolled in Carnegie-Mellon University. At that time Carnegie-Mellon did not allow women to major in engineering. Because the United States was involved in World War II, many of the male students were away at war. Therefore, the university allowed

Stephanie to take courses in chemistry and engineering. As with other young women of her generation, opportunities denied to them before the war became available to them during the war. The country needed more scientists. Science research at major universities and colleges reached an all-time high. Many women took advantage of the situation and chose to study science.

When Kwolek graduated from Carnegie-Mellon with a major in both chemistry and biology in 1946, she wanted to go to medical school. Going to medical school cost a great deal of money. Because her family was not able to help pay for a medical school education, Kwolek planned to work for a year to save enough money for the first year of medical school. She found a job at E. I. du Pont de Nemours and Company as a chemist. She soon discovered that she enjoyed being a chemist. Kwolek worked from 1946 to 1950 in Buffalo, New York, in the Rayon Department of DuPont. Then DuPont moved its Pioneering Research Laboratory to Wilmington, Delaware. Kwolek moved with the company and spent the next thirty-six years doing research in chemistry.

Life as a woman chemist was very difficult. At the end of the war, when the men returned home, most women scientists were encouraged to leave industry. Kwolek did not want to leave DuPont, even though the company did not promote her or give her raises. This lack of recognition continued despite the fact that her research team continued to produce a variety of innovative products.

Kwolek did her research in the part of chemistry known as polymer chemistry. A polymer is a string of small molecules that connect together to make very long chains. Examples of polymers occurring naturally include DNA, proteins, starch, and rubber. Before World War II, the only fibers available to make cloth were natural ones, like wool from sheep, cotton and flax from plants, and silk from silkworms. In 1939, near the beginning of World War II, a new material was produced purely through a chemical process. It was called nylon.

Nylon is a strong, hardwearing polymer, which does not rot or absorb water. Nylon became very popular. During the war, items made from nylon replaced those made from silk, such as women's stockings. Nylon joined the war effort as manufacturers quickly used this new material for parachutes. Making fibers and materials chemically in a laboratory gave birth to a completely new field of chemical research. The search for other ways to make different kinds of cloth and plastics was underway.

The chemists at DuPont participated in this search for the new fibers. Dacron polyester, Orlon acrylic, and Lycra spandex were some of the fabrics invented and produced by chemists at Dupont. Combining her love of science and her love of cloth and material, Kwolek joined the hunt for new fibers. Most chemical researchers were looking for polymers

Dr. Stephanie Kwolek is shown preparing a new polymer in the Pioneering Research Laboratory at The Dupont Company.

that they could spin into long threads at high temperatures. Kwolek chose to search for polymers that she could spin at room temperature. She led the way into low-temperature polymerization. She was one of the most important chemists in the nation because of her knowledge of polymers. One of her team's first discoveries was a fire-resistant fabric called Nomex.®2 Manufacturers made Nomex into protective clothing for firefighters.

In 1964, DuPont asked its scientists to find a material that was indestructable. Kwolek began experimenting with liquid crystals. *Liquid crystals* are polymer solutions that are different from ordinary polymers. In most polymers the molecules flow in a disorganized way. In liquid crystals the molecules all line up pointing in the same direction.3 In order to find the best polymer, Kwolek had to find the right solution of liquid crystals first. She spent many weeks trying different combinations of chemicals, searching for the right solution. One day she found a solution that did not act like any of the others. Most polymer solutions are transparent, like glass. The new one she found was like milk. Kwolek and her lab technicians spun the polymer and discovered that it was incredibly strong. At first, she did not believe how strong it was. She wondered if she and her team had made a mistake in recording the results from the strength tests. She performed the same experiment over and over. She tested the results again and again. Her coworkers knew she was a persistent and careful experimenter. The unique fiber Kwolek created became known as Kevlar.[®][4] Her search for this new fiber had started in 1966. She applied for the patent in 1971 when it went on the market. DuPont finally promoted her for this discovery.

DuPont had asked for a material like Superman's clothes. Kwolek and her team found it. Kevlar is used in many things requiring extra strength. It is five times stronger than steel and does not rust. Consumers can find Kevlar in items such as underwater cables, brake linings, belted tires, space vehicles, boats, and sailcloth. Carpenters use Kevlar in many of their building materials. One of its most famous uses is in bulletproof vests. It can be made into yarn, pulp, pellets, or thread. People who use axes and chainsaws use Kevlar gloves to keep from chopping off their fingers. The oil industry uses Kevlar ropes to keep platforms attached to the ocean bottom.

Stephanie Kwolek created more than just a new material. She discovered new solvents and new ways to spin the polymers. Kwolek's inventions opened up another area of chemistry aimed at developing more high-performance fibers. She holds many patents, especially those related to developing polymers at low temperatures. Her discoveries revolutionized the synthetics industry.[5]

Throughout her life and career as a chemist, Kwolek has received many awards. In 1978 she received the American Society for Metals Award. In

1980 the American Institute of Chemists awarded her the Chemical Pioneer Award. She also won the American Chemical Society's Award for Creative Invention. Although she retired from DuPont in 1986, she continued to receive honors and prizes. In 1992, she was inducted into the Engineering and Science Hall of Fame.

In 1995, Kwolek was inducted into the Inventors Hall of Fame. In 1996, President Clinton presented her with the National Medal of Technology. In 1997, she received the Perkin Medal, and in 1999 she was given the Lemelson-MIT lifetime Achievement Award.

Kwolek retired in 1986 and works as a consultant for DuPont.

Shirley Ann Jackson

9

Shirley Ann Jackson
Physicist

In the summer of 1999, Rensselaer Polytechnic Institute (RPI), a world-famous engineering university, elected an African-American woman to be its president. As a little girl, the new president of RPI, Shirley Ann Jackson, liked to collect insects. She had jars of bumblebees, hornets, and wasps. She experimented by putting the different kinds of insects together in the same jar to watch how they interacted with each other. She did other experiments with her insects. Sometimes she tried giving them a variety of foods, watching to see if certain foods made the insects act differently. Shirley's early interest in science continued throughout her life. She remains fascinated with the world around her and wants to know about its secrets.

Shirley Ann Jackson was born in Washington, D.C., in 1946. Shirley's parents, Beatrice Cosby Jackson and George H. Jackson, encouraged her interest in exploring living things.[1] Sometimes, her father helped her with her experiments. Together they grew molds and bacteria in the kitchen. Her father always told her "to aim for the stars so that you can reach the treetops, and at least you'll get off the ground."[2] Her mother inspired her by reading stories to her about other famous African Americans. Some of Shirley's favorite stories were about Benjamin Banneker, a mathematician and astronomer, Paul Laurence Dunbar, a poet, and Mary McLeod Bethune, an educator.

Shirley always liked going to school. Although she enjoyed all the subjects taught in her classes, one of her favorite subjects was mathematics. As a young child, she went to the Charles Young School. In those days the schools in Washington, D.C., were segregated—all the African-American children went to one school, while the white children went to other schools. In 1954, when Shirley was in middle school, the United States passed a law making segregation illegal in public schools. For a while Shirley attended an integrated school. Although the schools in Washington were supposed to be integrated, the high school she attended was not.

As in elementary school, she continued to enjoy all of the subjects taught in high school. She and several other young women formed a social and study club. They helped each other study all the subjects. An assistant principal at her high school encouraged Shirley to think about going to the Massachusetts Institute of Technology in Cambridge, Massachusetts (MIT). Most people know MIT for its rigorous academic program and its high expectations of its students. Being a student at MIT requires a great deal of determination to be successful. Shirley began classes there in September 1964. Because MIT had been a school primarily for white males, Shirley's parents worried about how a young black woman was going to survive in a school like that.

In 1964 approximately four thousand students attended MIT. Of these four thousand, only about a dozen were African-American students and about thirty were women students. There was only one other African-American woman in the class. The white women worked, studied, and played together, and did not include Shirley in their group. They completely ignored her. Shirley studied alone in her room every night. However, because she was able to do most of the homework problems alone and get good grades, some of the other students started to go to her for help.

Shirley Jackson earned good grades in all the difficult courses, but it was a lonely time for her. She focused her attention on her new love, physics.

Physics is the study of matter and energy. She enjoyed learning about how things in the universe worked. She chose physics as her major and set the course for her future career.

Despite all of the feelings of isolation, Jackson succeeded. She did not allow the loneliness to deter her. She did not spend every minute studying either. During her years at MIT, she volunteered at the Boston City Hospital. In addition, she worked with the administration of the university to help them find ways to recruit more minority students to MIT. She organized the Black Student Union and served as cochair for two years. In 1968 she graduated with a bachelor of science degree.

Many schools, including Harvard, Brown and the University of Chicago, invited her to join them for graduate work. However, she decided to stay on at MIT, where she studied theoretical solid state physics. She wanted to continue helping MIT recruit more African-American students. In 1973 Shirley Jackson became the first African-American woman to receive a doctoral degree from the Massachusetts Institute of Technology, and the second African-American women to receive a doctorate in physics in the United States.

During 1973 and 1974, she worked as a research associate in theoretical physics at the Fermi National Accelerator Laboratory in Batavia, Illinois. Here she did further research in particle physics. She studied how the basic particles of matter interact with each

Jackson was enrolled at MIT in 1964.

other. At age twenty-seven, she received the Scientist of the Year Award. A year later, in an interview for *Ebony* magazine, she said about her work, "I am trying to understand the fundamental interaction between the basic constituents of matter when they interact at high energy."[3]

Jackson spent a year traveling throughout Europe as a visiting science associate for the European Organization of Nuclear Research. While she was in Europe, she discovered that it was much easier to be an African-American woman scientist in Europe than in the United States. In Switzerland, for example, she was free to concentrate on science. In 1975 she returned to continue her work at the Fermi National Accelerator Laboratory. An offer to work on the Technical Staff of Bell Telephone Laboratories (Bell Labs) followed. At Bell Labs she changed her research focus from particle physics back to solid-state physics. Instead of studying the physics of single particles, she now studied what happened when atoms are grouped together to make a solid.

While at Bell Labs, she met and married Dr. Morris A. Washington, also a physicist. They have one son, Alan, who later attended Dartmouth College.

In 1991, after working at Bell Labs for sixteen years, the administration of Rutgers University appointed her as professor of physics. During her time at Rutgers, she continued to serve as a consultant for Bell Labs.

From 1995 to 1999 she became the first African American to serve on the Nuclear Regulatory Commission and was the first woman ever to chair the commission. While serving on the commission, she helped establish the International Nuclear Regulators Association, a group made up of the most senior nuclear regulatory officials from Canada, France, Germany, Japan, Spain, Sweden, the United Kingdom, and the United States. This group gathered to help nations examine issues of nuclear safety.

In 1998 The National Women's Hall of Fame inducted her into its membership for her "significant and profound contributions as a distinguished scientist and advocate for education, science and public policy."[4]

She has received many awards including: Outstanding Young Women of America in 1976 and 1981. She is listed in *American Men and Women of Science* and *Who's Who in the East,* and *Who's Who in Science and Technology.* Both the American Academy of Arts and Sciences and the American Physical Society elected her to be a Fellow. She holds ten honorary degrees.

In 1999, Rensselaer Polytechnic Institute elected her as their eighteenth president. On July 1, 2000, Rensselaer President Shirley Ann Jackson was named to the board of directors of the USX Corporation, a major worldwide producer of oil, natural gas, and steel products.

Flossie Wong-Staal

Flossie Wong-Staal
Medical Researcher

Flossie Wong-Staal is one of the world's leading authorities in the study of viruses.[1] She codiscovered the Human Immunodeficiency Virus (HIV). HIV is the name of the retrovirus that causes Acquired Immune Deficiency Syndrome (AIDS).

Flossie Wong was born in Kuangchou (Canton), China, on August 27, 1947. Her father, Sueh-fung Wong, was a businessman who bought and sold cloth from and to other countries. Her mother, Wei-chung, stayed at home as a homemaker. When Flossie was two years old, the Communists took control of China. At the time of the takeover, Flossie's father was on a business trip in Hong Kong, a then British owned and governed island off the coast of China. Because of the confusion and new restrictions brought about by the change in Chinese governments between 1947 and 1949, Sueh-fung Wong was unable to return to China or contact his family for a long time. It took three years before Flossie, her sister, brother, and mother were allowed to leave China to join Flossie's father. The family settled in Hong Kong in 1952.

Flossie's birth name was Yee Ching. When the family started their new life in Hong Kong, Yee Ching went to a Catholic school. The nuns at the school told Yee Ching's father that his daughter needed an English name. The nuns gave Sueh-fung Wong a list of names. He was supposed to choose a name for his daughter from the list. Yee-ching's father chose the name *Flossie*, which had been the name of a typhoon that had hit Hong Kong some days before.[2]

In high school as in many other English-speaking schools throughout the world at the time, students had to choose what track of courses they wanted to study. In Flossie's school, there were two choices: the liberal arts, such as history, literature, and philosophy or the sciences, such as chemistry and physics. Teachers encouraged the more intelligent students to take the science option. Flossie felt honored to be one of the students chosen for the science classes. She graduated from the all-girl's high school in 1965 and decided to go to college in the United States. Along with many of her friends from Hong Kong, she entered the University of California at Los Angeles (UCLA) in 1965.[3]

For her undergraduate work, Wong chose to study molecular biology. With the advanced technology available to scientists in the 1960s, especially the powerful electron microscope, it became possible to explore new areas of study. In one new field of genetics, scientists used these microscopes to identify parts of chromosomes called genes. Chromosomes are threadlike parts of DNA (deoxyribonucleic acid) found in the nuclei of plant or animal cells. DNA helps cells to reproduce. Chromosomes are responsible for hereditary traits, like hair and eye color. A gene is one of the tiny parts of the chromosome. Each gene is responsible for a specific aspect of a trait, such as blue eyes or brown eyes. Each gene has its own special place on the chromosome. The genes line up on the chromosome in a unique pattern. Therefore, each organism has its own DNA pattern.

Biologists learned how to change the structure of the genes, a process known as genetic engineering. As an undergraduate, Wong studied with scientists on the cutting edge of this new field of biology. Wong said, "It was a very exciting time, and I was just fascinated by it."[4] She graduated magna cum laude with a bachelor of arts degree in bacteriology from UCLA in 1968.

Wong stayed at UCLA to further her education in molecular biology. While there, she met Steven Staal, a medical student studying at the University of

California in San Diego (UCSD). They married in 1971. The following year, Flossie Wong-Staal graduated with a Ph.D. in molecular biology, was named Outstanding Woman Graduate of the Year, and gave birth to her daughter, Stephanie. She moved to San Diego to be with her husband and continued her studies at UCSD. When her husband moved to Bethesda, Maryland, to work at the National Institutes of Health (NIH), Flossie Wong-Staal followed. She joined Robert Gallo's lab at the National Cancer Institute in the 1970s. There she studied the genes of viruses that caused cancer in animals.

Viruses are very tiny. They cannot reproduce themselves unless they are inside a living cell. When a virus enters a human or animal cell and uses the host cell to help it reproduce, it often causes a disease to occur in the host plant or animal. Some viruses cause diseases like colds or the flu. Other viruses cause diseases like cancer. The viruses that cause cancer do so by "turning on" oncogenes. The *oncogene* is responsible for regulating cell growth by being "on" or "off." If oncogenes are turned on all the time, cells grow out of control. Cancerous tumors result when cells continue to grow and reproduce rapidly. Some viruses go through stages of development in a way that is different from most viruses. These viruses are called retroviruses, because they seem to work backward. As part of her first research at Robert Gallo's lab, Wong-Staal studied the retroviruses that caused cancer in monkeys and apes.

During the early 1980s, many researchers looked for the cause of AIDS (Acquired Immune Deficiency Syndrome). In 1981 the team of researchers at Gallo's lab isolated the first human cancer-causing retroviruses. In 1983, Gallo and Wong-Staal codiscovered Human Immunodeficiency Virus or HIV, the retrovirus that causes AIDS. A French researcher also discovered the same virus at the same time. In 1984, Wong-Staal cloned the virus's genetic material. *Cloning* is a method of making a copy of a DNA pattern in a laboratory. When a cell is cloned, it means that the two cells are identical in their DNA pattern. Scientists achieve this by rearranging the genes on the chromosome or by removing or adding genes. Cloning the retrovirus that caused AIDS was very important to the AIDS research community. Now scientists around the world could make large quantities of the retrovirus and use it for their research.

Wong-Staal studied the virus until she was able to identify the location of every gene on the chromosome. She also identified what each gene did. She continued analysis on retroviruses throughout the 1980s. She isolated each of the virus's genes and the extra genes that regulated the virus's growth. She found that some parts of the virus's genetic information kept changing. These changes in the genetic code made it very difficult for scientists to develop a vaccine to stop the spread of AIDS.

Flossie Wong-Staal continues to spend much of her time searching for methods to treat and prevent AIDS.

Wong-Staal's work made it possible for researchers to develop HIV tests. These tests are used to screen blood to make sure blood used in transfusions does not carry the HIV virus. These tests also help to identify people who are HIV positive or who have the HIV virus in their bodies but have not shown any of the symptoms of AIDS. Wong-Staal's work became the foundation for AIDS research. Between 1981 and 1988, scientists cited her studies more than any other scientist in the field. One can find references to her research in more than seven thousand different articles.[5] In 1985, when their second daughter, Caroline, was two years old, Flossie and Steven divorced.

Flossie Wong-Staal returned to California in 1990. She took a position as professor of medicine and biology at the University of California in San Diego. She holds the Florence Riford Chair in AIDS Research. That same year, the Institute for Scientific Information listed Wong-Staal as the top woman scientist of the 1980s and the fourth-ranking scientist under the age of forty-five. In 1994 the Center for AIDS Research (CFAR) was created. Wong-Staal became its first director and was elected to join the Institute of Medicine. Two years later, the University of California Board of Regents approved the formation of an AIDS Research Institute, known as ARI. The ARI includes the CFAR. The goal of ARI is to increase cooperation among the many educational institutions and private companies working on AIDS research. The ARI also hopes to increase the number of educational programs available to the general public on this topic.

Although it will be very difficult to develop a vaccine for AIDS because of the way the retrovirus reproduces, Wong-Staal continues to spend much of her time searching for methods to treat and prevent the disease. She says, "I think it's exciting to be part of a discovery, to know you're finding out things that have never been known before. If I had to advise young people going into science, I think that would be my major selling point, the excitement it generates."[6]

Chapter Notes

Chapter 1. Florence Bascom

1. Isabel Smith, *The Stone Lady* (Bryn Mawr, Pa.: Bryn Mawr College, 1981), p. 9.
2. Ibid., p. 23.
3. Jill S. Schneiderman, "A Life of Firsts: Florence Bascom," reprinted from *GSA Today*, July 1997, <www.geoclio.st.usm.edu/fbascom.html> (October 12, 1999).
4. Ibid.
5. Lois Barber Arnold, *Four Lives in Science: Women's Education in the Nineteenth Century* (New York: Schocken Books, 1984), pp. 114–123.
6. Smith, p. 32.

Chapter 2. Barbara McClintock

1. Harriet B. Creighton, "Recollections of Barbara McClintock's Cornell Years" in *The Dynamic Genome: Barbara McClintock's Ideas in the Century of Genetics*, ed. Nina Fedoroff and David Botstein (Cold Spring Harbor, N.Y.: Cold Spring Harbor Laboratory Press, 1992), p. 13.
2. Sharon Bertsch McGrayne, *Nobel Prize Women in Science: Their Lives, Struggles, and Momentous Discoveries* (New York: Birch Lane Press Book, 1993), p. 148.
3. Evelyn Fox Keller, *A Feeling for the Organism: The Life and Work of Barbara McClintock* (New York: W. H. Freeman and Company, 1983), p. 26.
4. Creighton, p. 17.
5. Keller, p. 86.
6. "Nobel in medicine recognizes McClintock's contributions," *Industrial Research*, Vol. 25 (November 1983), p. 49 (1), <http://web6.searchbank.com> (February 2, 1999).

7. Nina Federoff and David Botstein, *The Dynamic Genome: Barbara McClintock's Ideas in the Century of Genetics* (Cold Spring Harbor, N.Y.: Cold Spring Harbor Laboratory Press, 1992), p. 2.

8. Claudia Wallis, "Honoring a Modern Mendel; geneticist Barb McClintock, ignored for years, wins a Nobel," *Time*, vol. 122, October 24, 1983, p. 53, <http://web6.searchbank .com/html> (February 2, 1999).

Chapter 3. Maria Goeppert-Mayer

1. Joan Dash, *A Life of One's Own: Three Gifted Women and the Men They Married* (New York: Harper & Row, 1973), p. 238.

2. Sharon Bertsch McGrayne, *Nobel Prize Women in Science: Their Lives, Struggles, and Momentous Discoveries* (New York: Birch Lane Press Book, 1993), p. 182.

3. Ibid., p. 183.

4. Lisa Yount, *Contemporary Women Scientists* (New York: Facts On File, 1994), p.16.

5. McGrayne, p. 188.

6. Ibid., p. 193.

7. Karen Elise Johnson, *Maria Goeppert Mayer and the Development of the Nuclear Shell Model* (Ann Arbor, Mich.: University Microfilms International, 1986), p. 3.

Chapter 4. Grace Murray Hopper

1. Howard Bromberg, "Grace Murray Hopper: A Remembrance" (IEEE software, v. 9, May 1992), p. 103.

2. Marguerite Zientara, *The History of Computing: A Biographical Portrait of the Visionaries Who Shaped the Destiny of the Computer Industry* (Framingham, Mass.: CW Communications, Inc., 1981), p. 52.

3. Ibid., p. 52.

4. Lisa Yount, *Contemporary Women Scientists* (New York: Facts On File, 1994), p. 27.

5. Elizabeth Dickason, "Remembering Grace Murray Hopper: A Legend in Her Own Time," <http://www.norfolk.navy.mil/chips/grace_hopper/file2.htm>(October 12,1999).

6. Philip Schieber "Grace Hopper Celebration of Women in Computing," *The OCLC Newsletter*, March/April 1987, No. 167, <http://www.cs.yale.edu/~tap/Files/hopper-wit.html> (October 12,1999).

7. Zientara, p. 52.

8. Schieber, op. cit. <http://www.cs.yale.edu/~tap/Files/Hopper-story.html>.

9. Ibid.

10. Dickason, op. cit.

Chapter 5. Rachel Carson

1. Marcia Myers Bonta, *American Women Afield: Writings by Pioneering Women Naturalists* (College Station, Tex.: Texas A&M University, 1995), p. 236.

2. Linda Lear, *Rachel Carson: Witness for Nature* (New York: Henry Holt and Company, 1997), pp. 43–45.

3. Benjamin Shearer and Barbara Shearer, *Notable Women in the Life Sciences: A Biographical Dictionary* (Westport, Conn.: Greenwood Press, 1996), p. 59.

4. Ibid., p. 60.

5. Rachel Carson, *Silent Spring* (Boston: Houghton Mifflin Co., 1961), p. 42.

6. Bonta, p. 271.

Chapter 6. Chien-Shiung Wu

1. Sharon Bertsch McGrayne, *Nobel Prize Women in Science: Their Lives, Struggles, and Momentous Discoveries* (New York: Birch Lane Press Book, 1993), p. 260.

2. McGrayne, p. 263.

3. Iris Noble, *Contemporary Women Scientists of America* (New York: Julian Messner, 1979), p. 83.

4. Lisa Yount, *Contemporary Women Scientists* (New York: Facts On File, 1994), p. 44.

5. Noble, p. 81.

6. Autumn Stanley, *Mothers and Daughters of Invention: Notes for a Revised History of Technology* (New Brunswick, N.J.: Rutgers University Press, 1993), p. 383.

Chapter 7. Rosalyn Sussman Yalow

1. Eugene Straus, M.D., *Rosalyn Yalow: Nobel Laureate: Her Life and Work in Medicine* (New York: Plenum Trade, 1998), p. 258.

2. Rosalyn S. Yalow (autobiography) <http://www.nobel.se/laureates/medicine-1977-3-autobio.html> (September 29, 1999).

3. Benjamin F. Shearer and Barbara S. Shearer, eds., *Notable Women in the Life Sciences: A Biographical Dictionary* (Westport, Conn.: Greenwood Press, 1996), p. 409.

4. Dennis Overbye, "Rosalyn Yalow: Lady Laureate of the Bronx," *Discover*, June, 1982, p. 42.

5. Yalow, op. cit.

6. Yalow, op. cit.

7. Shearer and Shearer, p. 409.

8. Yalow, op. cit.

9. Straus, p. 258.

Chapter 8. Stephanie Louise Kwolek

1. Inventure Place: Stephanie Louise Kwolek, <www.invent.org/book-text/64.html> (December 12, 2000).

2. The Lemelson-MIT Program's Invention Dimension: Stephanie L. Kwolek, <web.mit.edu/invent/www/inventorsI-Q/kwolek.html> (December 21, 1998).

3. Chemical Heritage Foundation: Perkin Medal, Stephanie Lindbergh Kwolek, <www.chemheritage.org/perkin/Kwolek/kwolek.html> (October 22, 1999).

4. The Great Idea Finder: Stephanie L. Kwolek, <www.ideafinder.com/history/inventors/kwolek.htm> (December 12, 2000).

5. Lemelson-MIT: Program Tech Mall, <www.8techmall .com/techdocs/TS990423-6.html> (March 1, 2001).

Chapter 9. Shirley Ann Jackson

1. Rensselaer.MAG: "Aim for the Stars," <www.rpi.edu/ dept/NewsComm/Magazine/sept99/jackson_1.html> (October 18, 1999).
2. Ibid.
3. "Nuclear Physicist at Fermi Lab," Ebony (Chicago: Johnson Publishing Co., 1994), November, p. 115.
4. National Women's Hall of Fame, <www.greatwomen .org/Jackson.htm> (October 18, 1999).

Chapter 10. Flossie Wong-Staal

1. Helen Zia and Susan B. Gall, eds., *Asian American Biography* (New York: UXL, 1995), p. 375.
2. *Notable Asian Americans* (Detroit: Gale Research Inc., 1995), p. 418.
3. Emilio Alvarez and Ann Crystal Angeles, "Science Superstar," *National Geographic World*, June 1993, p. 25.
4. Lisa Yount, *Contemporary Women Scientists* (New York: Facts On File, 1994), p. 109.
5. Abigail Grissom, "Top 10 Women Scientists of the '80s: Making a Difference," *The Scientist* <www.the-scientist .library.upenn.edu/yr1990/oct/researh1> (October 22, 1999).
6. University of California, San Diego Catalog School of Medicine, <http://cybermed,uscd.edu/Catalog/profiles/wong .html> (October 2, 1999).

Further Reading

Cooney, Miriam P. *Celebrating Women in Mathematics and Science.* Reston, Va.: National Council of Teachers of Mathematics, 1996.

Dash, Joan. *The Triumph of Discovery: Women Scientists Who Won the Nobel Prize.* Englewood Cliffs, N.J.: Julian Messner, 1990.

DeAngelis, Gina. *Female Firsts in Their Fields: Science & Medicine.* Philadelphia: Chelsea House Publishers, 1999.

Hacker, Carlotta. *Nobel Prize Winners.* New York: Crabtree Publishing Company, 1998.

Hacker, Carlotta. *Scientists.* New York: Crabtree Publishing Company, 1998.

Heiligman, Deborah. *Barbara McClintock: Alone in Her Field.* New York: Scientific American Books for Young Readers, 1994.

Lindop, Laurie. *Scientists and Doctors.* New York: Twenty-First Century Books, 1997.

Sirch, Willow Ann. *Eco-women: Protectors of the Earth.* Golden, Colo.: Fulcrum Kids, 1996.

Stille, Darlene R. *Extraordinary Women Scientists.* Chicago: Childrens Press, 1995.

Yount, Lisa. *Twentieth-Century Women Scientists.* New York: Facts On File, 1996.

Internet Addresses

4,000 Years of Women in Science
<http://www.astr.ua.edu/4000ws/>
An inventory of female astronomers, physicists, and other scientists with biographies, photos, and other references. See Biographies to search by name.

Distinguished Women of Past and Present
<http://www.distinguishedwomen.com>
See Search by Name to find out more about the women scientists in this book.

Female Nobel Prize Laureates
<http://www.almaz.com/nobel/women.html>

Index